LOUISE JEFFERSON is an Australian freelance photographer
now living and working in London.

ROBERT BALLAGH is a painter and designer whose design work has included
Irish postage stamps and banknotes, and the set of *Riverdance*.

DUBLIN

THEN AND NOW

SCENES FROM A REVOLUTIONARY CITY

DUBLIN
THEN AND NOW
SCENES FROM A REVOLUTIONARY CITY

LOUISE JEFFERSON
FOREWORD BY ROBERT BALLAGH

THE BREHON PRESS
BEYOND THE PALE PUBLICATIONS
BELFAST

First published 2006 by The Brehon Press Ltd
1A Bryson Street, Belfast BT5 4ES, Northern Ireland

and

Beyond the Pale BTP Publications Ltd
Unit 2.1.2 Conway Mill, 5-7 Conway Street
Belfast BT13 2DE, Northern Ireland

Original photography © 2006 Louise Jefferson
Foreword © 2006 Robert Ballagh

ISBN: 1 905474 08 3

Design by December Publications
Printed and bound by J.H. Haynes & Co Ltd., Sparkford

For Molly who left,
and for Paris who came back

Foreword

Robert Ballagh

'All has changed, changed utterly, a terrible beauty is born.'

What a perfect way to introduce this remarkable collection of photographs of Dublin, both old and new.

Now, I know that what William Butler Yeats had in mind when he wrote his few lines about Easter 1916 was not the physical transformation of his native city but rather the psychological condition of its citizens after the trauma of the Easter Rising and its aftermath. Nonetheless, the sentiment expressed is relevant when considering the many changes wrought to Ireland's capital over the last century.

The archive photographs of a damaged Dublin in 1916 are instructive in that they graphically illustrate the lengths to which the authorities were prepared to go in order to suppress the insurrection. James Connolly, a convinced socialist, believed that a capitalist government would not destroy capitalist property in Ireland. The reality was that the British government of the time was not only capitalist but also imperialist and consequently was not prepared to tolerate a 'stab in the back' whilst waging imperial war in Europe. The rebellion had to be brutally suppressed at any cost. Dublin's city centre was quickly reduced to rubble by the gunship 'Helga' – a 1916 version of 'shock and awe'.

Yet, in spite of such destruction, the city's wounds were quickly repaired. For example, one of the archive photos shows the GPO already rebuilt in 1921. This reality enabled my father to boast that he had grown up in the city that was exactly described by that great cerebral cartographer James Joyce, and I, in spite of the passage of time, found I could make the same claim.

Sadly, I'm afraid the unchanging nature of Dublin for such a long period was due, not to enlightened architectural preservation, but rather to political, economic and cultural paralysis.

Terence Brown, in his book *Ireland: A Social and Cultural History*, asked how 'a revolution fought on behalf of exhilarating ideals, which had been crystallised in the heroic crucible of the Easter Rising could have led to the establishment of an Irish state notable for a stultifying lack of social, cultural and economic ambition'.

James Plunkett, the author of *Strumpet City*, provided a partial answer when he observed that 'the country's leaders, their work of revolution completed, reacted into conservative policies and an extraordinary obsessive obscurantism'.

Indeed, one of those same leaders remarked: 'We were the most conservative of revolutionaries.' Again to quote Terence Brown, 'No architectural splendours can be pointed to as expressions of a confident, assertive self-regard in a society persuaded of its own newly independent traditional strengths.'

So, Ireland and especially her capital city remained unchanged and underdeveloped until economic circumstances forced the country's leaders to adopt a radical shift in the way the economy was managed. When Eamon de Valera was replaced as Taoiseach by Séan Lemass in 1959, new policies were set in train that abandoned the failed economic strategy of an earlier age and instead invited foreign capital to invest in Ireland. One result of this development was the tearing down of many old buildings in Dublin and their replacement by modern office blocks to house the new businesses. This so-called 'progress' in the 1960s and 1970s, where large tracts of Dublin's architectural heritage were thoughtlessly sacrificed on the altar of profit to make way for speculative office blocks, was well described in Frank McDonald's book *The Destruction of Dublin*. On the other hand, there was some resistance; architectural students occupied threatened Georgian buildings and lobby groups emerged, like the Irish Georgian Society, eventually creating a public mood that would not tolerate such vandalism today.

That said, within a decade or so, Dublin was so changed that my own children would have been hard pressed to recognise in their own city many aspects of the Dublin of Joyce. And more change was to come; with the arrival of the Celtic Tiger, hardly a street in the capital now remains unaltered. In the last decade Dublin's skyline has begun to resemble a forest of cranes, and as the fabric of the city has been transformed beyond recognition, so too has the composition of its citizens. Not so long ago Dubliners were a fairly homogeneous lot; not so now! Today's Dubliners can be not only Irish but also African, Chinese, Eastern European and many other nationalities who have arrived on our shores determined to share in our economic good fortune. These are the contrasts which have been skilfully exploited in this book.

I suppose the most striking change, illustrated in several photographs, is the replacement of Nelson's Pillar by the Spire. When I was a kid, the climb to the top of the Pillar was the best value in town. For a few old pennies you could view the whole city spread out before you like a giant map. When it came down in 1966, I have to admit that I was somewhat disappointed, not, I hasten to add, by the demise of the 'one-eyed adulterer', but rather by the loss of a favourite architectural feature. I always believed that a better solution would have been to retain Francis Johnson's beautiful Doric column, but to replace Nelson with a symbolic flame like the one held aloft in New York harbour by Liberty herself. Also, I'm afraid I am not convinced by its replacement, the Spire. At the risk of sounding contradictory, I feel that it's rather 'pointless', but then, maybe that's an appropriate description for the Ireland of today! Most public monuments commemorate or celebrate somebody or something, so you would expect a self-confident society to mark its own history, culture and achievements on such a prominent city centre site. In Dublin, the authorities decided, instead, to erect a very tall structure that says absolutely nothing about anything!

The other contrast that is underlined by the clever juxtaposition of photographs is the transformation of the depicted. Gone, of course, are the British troops of the 1916-1921 period, but their replacements tell us much about contemporary Ireland. One archive photograph showing victorious British troops with a captured rebel flag in front of the Parnell monument is humorously set beside a gathering of modern-day invaders: GAA supporters from the rebel county Cork. In others troop carriers are contrasted with an assortment of vehicles carrying tourists.

However, perhaps the most significant juxtaposition occurs when we view the archive photo of the surrender of Padraig Pearse to General Lowe beside a photograph of Moore Street today. Here our past rubs shoulder with our cosmopolitan future. It's unlikely that the new Dubliners who shop in Moore Street are aware of the history that survives in the very fabric of the city, yet their successful integration into Irish society requires that we all embrace the democratic vision of the men and women who fought and finally surrendered outside 16 Moore Street. That vision is encapsulated in the Proclamation of the Republic, a remarkable democratic document rightly belonging in the pantheon of human progress alongside Jefferson's declaration of American independence and the declaration of the first convention of the French Revolution.

Robert Ballagh
Dublin
April 2006

Author's Introduction

My maternal grandma, Molly Horrigan, was from Dublin. After marrying a British soldier stationed in Dublin, she was given just 24 hours to leave. She never returned. This was just prior to the Easter Rising of 1916. They set up home in Glasgow, where my mother grew up very tough in the midst of sectarian violence. My (by now Catholic) grandfather was sent to fight in the trenches in France, 1914-1918. I never knew him, as he died some time later from gas inhalation he'd endured there.

When I was a child grandma always told me that she would take me to Dublin one day. She didn't and I couldn't know then that she never would. But that promise stayed with me into adulthood and is part of what led me eventually to grandma's home city.

After leaving my home in Australia to live in London a few years ago, I thought I would at last have my visit and study my Irish ancestry. I read many books with photos of the British occupied, oppressed and poverty-stricken Dublin grandma must have grown up in. I wanted to show to the world the 'Then and Now' of this utterly changed city and, being a photographer, I hit on the idea of this book.

I went over and took a few pictures and sent some samples of what I was doing to Beyond the Pale Publications. I waited nervously and, incredibly, I received an email from them on 29 January, grandma's birthday, to say they were very interested. I was elated and went skipping down the street, yelling to the sky, 'We're having a book of Dublin published, grandma!' I'm sure she heard me; certainly others in the street did and gave me strange looks.

So my quest began in earnest. I've now made many visits to Dublin and it's been a very enlightening journey.

After I decided which photographs of Dublin between the Easter Rising of 1916 and the Civil War of 1921-22 I wanted to use, the next task was to go back to the streets depicted and photograph them today. Finding the exact spot I was looking for was not always easy, but a wonderful moment when I did. Once, I was searching up and down Grafton Street, looking for the spot where the IRA men had been photographed walking in 1922 with their hats and guns (see cover and page 98). I'd almost given up, when suddenly there was the spot – and with three young men with comic Irish hats and cameras in the exact same place. I almost dropped the camera with excitement, but got a fantastic shot. I was standing next to the statue of Molly Malone and I smiled at her. We both walked the streets of Dublin, she with her barrow, me with my camera.

Another time I was in Henry Street, looking at an old photo and trying to line up where British artillery had blown the GPO to pieces, when an elderly man, who'd been watching me, came up and showed me the exact spot. We had a good old chat. I've met a lot of interesting people in this way, all looking forward to seeing my book.

Even when I found the spot, it wasn't always easy to get the picture I wanted. Getting a crowd of people round Parnell's Monument in O'Connell Street was quite a challenge, as this is now on a busy traffic island. I had tried several times to get people to stand there, but it was only a few people, like a small family, which didn't have the impact I wanted. So when I heard there was an All-Ireland Hurling Final at Croke Park, I knew this could be the opportunity. I knew the supporters would all be in O'Connell Street near the Royal Dublin and Gresham hotels. So I planned a visit to Dublin especially on that weekend. I spoke to a group of young guys wearing Cork colours, asked them if they wanted to be in a book and, laughing, they obliged. I pleaded with them to wait and tore around collecting other Cork supporters, looking for ones with flags, ushering them along, with the young guys beckoning, By now others were joining in out of curiosity and I had a good crowd, flags and all. To take the picture I had to stand where the traffic was flowing, but I couldn't keep waiting for the lights to change and risk my group wandering away, so I plonked myself in the middle of the road and wouldn't move till I'd finished. Cars were furiously honking their horns, but short of running me over, they had to wait. When I'd finished, my supporters all let out a huge cheer. I was sweating like anything with the effort of it all, but ecstatic. I knew I had The Picture (see page 65). It was only later that I realised that the Cork flag was upside down!

On another occasion, I'd planned to get the picture at Leinster House where the statue of Queen Victoria was taken down. But it was the weekend and the grounds were closed. I pleaded with the guard to let me in, but he said he couldn't. I could see if I walked round and went through the Museum of Ireland and out the back that I would be in a good position if I looked through the railings. Oh no! There was building going on (not on weekends) but it was completely fenced off. I pleaded with the museum porter to let me go through, but he said he couldn't. Then I noticed a big gate that would lead me through which said 'Building Site, Strictly No Admittance'. I stared at it gloomily, then noticed a bell, and pressed it and lo, the huge gate slowly opened. I couldn't see nor hear anybody, so I innocently walked in, up to my spot, took the picture and left (see page 111). I guess I'll never know if anybody let me in, but I smiled and waved in case someone had taken pity on me.

While walking round the bustling streets of Dublin today, I try to imagine grandma running round the slum streets of Dublin a century ago, in her bare feet (she'd told me). I felt such an affinity with her and Dublin that I knew I'd finally come home to my Irish roots.

And not just me! My actress daughter Paris always tells people, 'My mum can do anything', and her faith in me has helped so much with this (my first) book. As the book goes to press, Paris has been given the lead in a play at Dublin's Gate Theatre. The circle has turned: granddaughter and great-granddaughter back in Molly Horrigan's city.

Louise Jefferson
London
April 2006

Sackville Street, April 1916.
General Post Office, headquarters of republican insurgents,
under fire from British artillery.
© *Imperial War Museum*

O'Connell Street, with Parnell monument in foreground.

Sackville Street, May 1916.
General Post Office and ruins after bombardment.
© *National Library of Ireland*

O'Connell Street, with General Post Office in background.

Sackville Street, May 1916.
Aftermath of British artillery bombardment.
© *National Library of Ireland*

O'Connell Street, with statue of Thomas Davis in foreground.

Arran Quay and Church Street, May 1916.
British soldiers clearing up after fighting.
© *National Museum of Ireland*

Arran Quay.

Henry Street, May 1916, with Nelson's Pillar in centre.
© *National Library of Ireland*

DUBLIN THEN...

Henry Street, with The Spire in centre.

Sackville Street, May 1916.
Newspaper vendor outside General Post Office.
© *RTE Stills Library*

O'Connell Street. Gardaí and others outside General Post Office.

Sackville Street and Bachelors Walk, May 1916.
© *RTE Stills Library*

D U B L I N   T H E N . . .

O'Connell Street and Bachelors Walk.

16 Sackville Place, off Sackville Street, 1916.
A railway boiler converted into an armoured car by British forces.
© *RTE Stills Library*

Sackville Place.

Sackville Street, 1916.
Building of Clery and Co., damaged in shelling.
© *RTE Stills Library*

O'Connell Street. Clery and Co.

Sackville Street, 1916.
YMCA building damaged by British shelling.
© *RTE Stills Library*

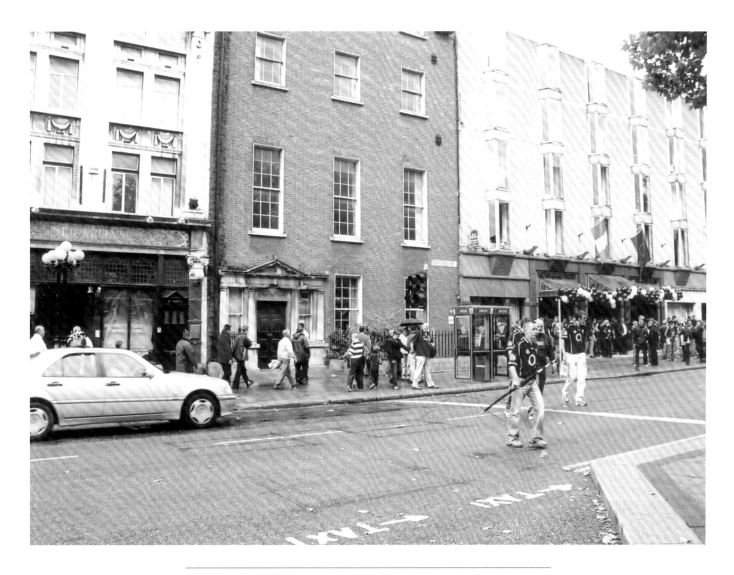

O'Connell Street, with Royal Dublin Hotel on right.

Eden Quay, May 1916.
Shelled from British gunboat, 'Helga'.

Eden Quay.

Sackville Street and Eden Quay, May 1916,
after shelling from British gunboat, 'Helga'.
© *RTE Stills Library*

O'Connell Street and Eden Quay,
with statue of O'Connell in foreground.

Lower Sackville Street and Eden Quay, May 1916,
after shelling from British gunboat, 'Helga'.

O'Connell Street and Eden Quay,
with statue of O'Connell to left.

Inside the General Post Office, April 1916,
with rebels under heavy artillery fire.
© *National Museum of Ireland*

Inside the General Post Office, O'Connell Street.

Sackville Street, 1916.
Damaged General Post Office
with British soldier on guard.

O'Connell Street.
A tourist outside the General Post Office.

Moore Street, republican
headquarters, April 1916.
Padraig Pearse surrenders to
General Lowe.
© *RTE Stills Library*

Moore Street.

Kilmainham Gaol, May 1916.
Execution of Padraig Pearse.
© *National Museum of Ireland*

Kilmainham Gaol.
Memorial to executed leaders of 1916 Rising.

Eden Quay and Sackville Street, 1916, after shelling.
© *RTE Stills Library*

Eden Quay and O'Connell Street.

Kilmainham Gaol, 1916.
Rebel prisoners.

DUBLIN THEN . . .

Kilmainham Gaol, now a museum, with tourists.

Kilmainham Lane, beside Kilmainham Gaol, 1916.
Two republican prisoners being brought to jail
under armed guard.
© *RTE Stills Library*

DUBLIN THEN...

Kilmainham Lane.

Northumberland Road, 1916.
Eamon De Valera (marked with an X) and
prisoners being taken from Boland's Mill to jail.
© *RTE Stills Library*

Northumberland Road.

Eden Quay, 1916.
Republican prisoners being taken to Frongoch Camp, Wales.
© *RTE Stills Library*

Eden Quay.

O'Connell Bridge, May 1916.
Republican prisoner under armed escort.
© *Imperial War Museum*

O'Connell Bridge, with jogger.

Liberty Hall, 1916.
Headquarters of Irish Transport and General Workers' Union
and Irish Citizen Army, damaged in fighting.
© *National Library of Ireland*

Liberty Hall.

Sackville Street, 1916.
British soldiers with captured republican flag
at Parnell monument.
© *National Museum of Ireland*

O'Connell Street, with Cork hurling supporters.

Westland Row Station; crowds welcome home republican
prisoners released from Frongoch Camp, Wales.
© *National Library of Ireland*

Pearse Station, Pearse Street.

Dublin, Black and Tan patrol, 1920.

Dublin, amphibious tour bus.

Dublin, 1921.
British soldiers search a car.
© *National Museum*

Dublin. Tourists in horse-drawn carriage.

Kildare Street, 1921.
British troops search buildings.
© *RTE Stills Library*

Kildare Street. National Museum on the right.

Sackville Street, 1920.
British armoured car.

O'Connell Street. Tourist bus.

Sackville Street, 1921.
Skirmish between crowd and British armoured patrol.
General Post Office on left, being rebuilt.
© *RTE Stills Library*

O'Connell Street, with General Post Office on left
and statue of James Larkin on right.

Sackville Street, 1921.
British army rounding up rebels.
General Post Office on left, now rebuilt.
© *RTE Stills Library*

O'Connell Street with General Post Office.

Sackville Street, 1921.
British army vehicle makes its way after a disturbance.
© *RTE Stills Library*

O'Connell Street, with O'Connell statue in distance.

Dublin, 1921.
British soldier searches civilian.
© *RTE Stills Library*

Dublin businessmen on St Stephen's Green.

College Green, 1921.
Disabled British army vehicle.
© *RTE Stills Library*

College Green.
Sinn Féin parade.

Dawson Street, 1921.
Royal Irish Constabulary auxiliaries on duty at Mansion House.
© *RTE Stills Library*

Dawson Street.

Wellington Barracks, 1920.
British soldiers.
© *RTE Stills Library*

Collins Barracks (formerly Wellington Barracks).
Irish soldiers.

Dublin, May 1921.
Custom House burned by IRA.
© *National Museum of Ireland*

Dublin.
The Custom House.

Dublin, May 1921.
Custom House burning.

Dublin.
Custom House from Burgh Quay.

Beresford Place.
Black and Tans take IRA prisoners outside Custom House.
© *RTE Stills Library*

Beresford Place.

Dublin Castle, 1922.
The last British soldiers leave.
© *RTE Stills Library*

Dublin Castle.
Sinn Féin colour party at parade.

Grafton Street, 1922.
IRA patrol during Civil War.
© *Hutton Getty Images*

Grafton Street.

Upper Sackville Street, June 1922.
Pro-Treaty troops attack republican stronghold during Civil War.
© *Guardian Newsroom*

O'Connell Street, with Royal Dublin Hotel on right.

Inns Quay, June 1922.
Four Courts ablaze during Civil War.

Inns Quay.
Four Courts.

Inns Quay, June 1922.
Four Courts ablaze during Civil War.

Inns Quay.
Four Courts.

Sackville Street, June 1922.
Pro-Treaty troops attack anti-Treaty stronghold.
Nelson's Pillar to left.
© *Guardian Newsroom*

O'Connell Street.
The Spire on left.

Sackville Street, 1922.
Ruins of Gresham Hotel.
© RTE Stills Library

O'Connell Street.
Gresham Hotel.

Leinster House, 22 July 1948.
Removal of statue of Queen
Victoria before declaration of
Irish Republic.

Leinster House.